12 Strategies Understanding Word Problems

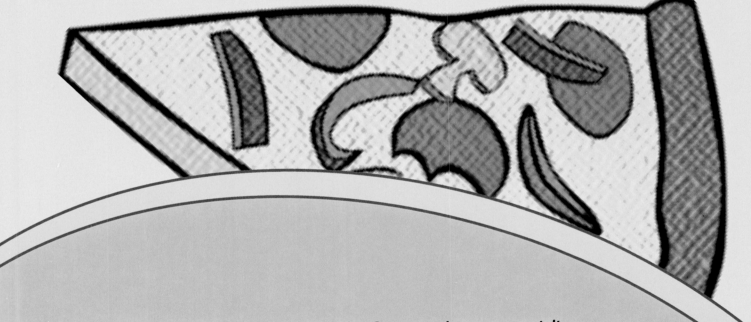

A Quick Read™ resource guide for teachers, providing practical strategies to help increase student understanding and success with word problems.

by Christine King

This book is dedicated to John.
Thank you for always supporting me,
Providing me with critical feedback, and
being one of my loudest cheerleaders.

**"I just can't get the word problems!
The rules don't always work like with regular math."**
– Anonymous, Frustrated Student

Contents

About this Book

"They just can't get the word problems!"
– Anonymous, Frustrated Teacher

I have heard this statement in various forms during my years as a classroom teacher and while working as an educational consultant. I myself have probably made the same statement at one point or another. This book is about providing hope. Hope to new and experienced educators alike. Hope that we can help all of our students become better at solving word problems.

This book outlines 12 classroom strategies aligned to the Common Core State Standards' Mathematical Practices. The strategies will help you get to the core of solving word problems which is — **understanding the problem**. Sprinkled throughout this book are "Ponder This!" opportunities, which are meant to be used to facilitate discussions around what research reveals about how students solve word problems and why they struggle.

This book is meant to be a quick, yet powerful read that will stir you to action, accepting that solving word problems are challenging cognitive endeavors. Research shows how we can use strategies that promote and build understanding through the use of comprehension, visualization, segmenting, paraphrasing, and representing strategies to help students become better problem solvers. This book will challenge you to slow down the problem solving process and move way from "answer-getting" techniques.

"50% - 70% of student difficulties with solving word problems occur between processes 1 to 3."

Newman's Error Analysis Levels	
Processes used to solve a problem	**Action at each stage**
1. Reading	Reading the problem
2. Comprehension	Comprehending what is read
3. Transformation	Carrying out a transformation from the words of the problem to the selection of an appropriate mathematical strategy
4. Process	Applying the process skills demanded by the selected strategy
5. Encoding	Encoding the answer in an acceptable written form

Adapted from Newman, A. (1983) The Newman language of mathematics kit. Sydney, NSW: Harcourt, Brace & Jovanovich

Adapted Newman's Error Analysis for Problem Solving

Processes used to solve a problem	Action at each stage
1. Decoding	Reading the problem fluently
2. Comprehension	Comprehending what is read
3. Visualizing	Making a mental picture and sketch or diagram of the situation
4. Transformation	Carrying out a transformation from the words in the problem to the selection of an appropriate mathematical strategy
5. Process	Applying the process skills demanded by the selected strategy
6. Encoding	Encoding the answer in an acceptable written form
7. Alternative Method	Showing how to solve in another way

Strategies Overview

Strategy Name	Addressing	Mathematical Practice
1. Word Problem Puzzle	Comprehension	#1: Make sense of problems and persevere in solving them
2. What is the Question?	Understanding the Context	#3: Construct viable arguments and critique the reasoning of others
3. A Line at a Time	Chunking/Segmenting	#2: Reason abstractly and quantitatively
4. State in Your Own Words	Paraphrasing	#1: Make sense of problems and persevere in solving them
5. Make a Mental Movie	Visualization	#6: Attend to precision
6. Identifying the Math	Conceptual Understanding	#4: Model with mathematics
7. Make a Mathematical Sketch	Representation	#4: Model with mathematics
8. Make a Math Model	Representation	#4: Model with mathematics
9. Worked Solutions	Imitation	#3: Construct viable arguments and critique the reasoning of others
10. Cloze Word Problem	Comprehension	#1: Make sense of problems and persevere in solving them
11. Numbers, Numbers, Numbers	Contextualization	#2: Reason abstractly and quantitatively
12. This and That, and Them	Monitoring/Clarifying	#1: Make sense of problems and persevere in solving them

#1: Word Problem Puzzle

Benefits: Prompts students to read and make sense of word problems. Encourages discourse. Builds an understanding of the structure of word problems.

Task: Cut word problem into strips; each strip is one sentence from the problem. Students have to make sense of the word problem by placing the sentence strips in order.

COMPREHENSION

Mathematical Practice #1: Make sense of problems and persevere in solving them.

Put this word problem in order.

Tina has 6 fewer pieces of candy than Tony.

Tina also has some Skittles.

How many pieces of candy does Tina have?

Tony has 18 Skittles.

PONDER THIS!

Students can solve most one-step problems but have extreme difficulty trying to solve **nonstandard problems,** problems requiring multi-steps, or problems with extraneous information. Teachers must avoid introducing students to techniques that work for one-step problems but do not generalize to multi-step problems, such as the association of "key" words with particular operations (Carpenter, et al., 1981).

DISCUSSION OPPORTUNITY

#2: What is the Question?

Benefits: Allows for multiple levels of entry based upon a student's understanding of the context. Helps students identify mathematical concepts given in real life situations.

Task: Take a word problem and remove the question. Students have to come up with questions that could be answered based upon the context or situation.

UNDERSTANDING THE CONTEXT

Mathematical Practice #3: Construct viable arguments and critique the reasoning of others.

Can you figure out some math questions that could be asked and answered given this situation?

"Anya, guess what?" said Julie, "I just went shopping at the mall and got some new clothes."

"What did you get?" asked Anya.

"I bought a pair of jeans for $39.99, a belt for $12.99, two tops for $19.99 each, and a pair of shoes for $50.00. And I had a coupon, so I got 10% off everything."

#3: A Line at a Time

Benefits: Reveals student's abilities to connect ideas from one sentence to the next. Slows down the process of "answer-getting" and encourages **sense-making** by segmenting word problems.

Task: Reveal a word problem one sentence at a time. As each line is revealed have students discuss and visualize the information and how that information connects to what they already know.

CHUNKING/SEGMENTING

Visualize!

Nikki, Cecilia, and Donnell were riding their bicycles at the park.

Visualize!

Nikki decided to rest after they had been riding for about one mile.

Visualize!

Cecilia and Donnell decided to continue on for another two miles before turning back to meet up with Nikki.

Mathematical Practice #2: Reason abstractly and quantitatively.

Show Your Thinking!

If Nikki figured out the total number of miles that she and her friends rode that day, what would she have said?

PONDER THIS!

Students tend to speed read through a problem and immediately begin to manipulate the numbers involved in some fashion (often irrationally). Mathematics teachers need to encourage students to use "slow down" mechanisms that can help them concentrate on understanding the problem, its context, and what is being asked (Kantowski, 1981).

DISCUSSION OPPORTUNITY

#4: State in Your Own Words

Benefits: Allows students to make sense of a word problem without repeating the problem word for word. Helps students build their vocabulary as they associate terms.

Task: Students have to paraphrase a word problem. Certain words are **highlighted**. These words cannot be used when retelling the word problem.

PARAPHRASING

Mathematical Practice #1:
Make sense of problems and persevere in solving them.

You have 100 points. Paraphrase the word problem. You will lose 10 points each time you use one of the bolded words.

Willow Smith is **roughly two years** younger than her **brother** Jaden. Her oldest brother, **Trey**, is about six years older than Jaden. Willow's birthday is on **Halloween**. How old will **Willow** be when Trey turns 21?

#5: Make a Mental Movie

Benefits: Strengthening ability to connect problems to real life contexts and tap into their prior knowledge. Promotes discussion on different ways to see a situation.

Task: Students create a mental picture of a word problem. They will share, compare, and synthesize what they saw.

VISUALIZATION

Mathematical Practice #6: Attend to precision.

Create a mental movie of this word problem, then share what you saw.

> Amir is having a birthday party at McDonald's. His mother invited 10 of his friends. She ordered two hamburgers, one bag of French Fries and an apple juice for each of the children. If every item is from the "Dollar Menu", how much money did Amir's mother have to pay, excluding tax?

"If I can't picture it, I can't understand it." (Einstein)

PONDER THIS!

Research has shown that **mathematics texts contain more concepts per sentence** and paragraph than any other type of text. They are written in a very compact style; each sentence contains a lot of information, with little redundancy. The text can contain words as well as numeric and non-numeric symbols to decode. In addition, a page may be laid out in such a way that the eye must travel in a different pattern than the traditional left-to-right. There may also be graphics that must be understood for the text to make sense; these may sometimes include information that is intended to add to the comprehension of a problem but instead may be distracting. Finally, **many texts are written above the grade level** for which they are intended (Barton & Heidema, 2002).

DISCUSSION OPPORTUNITY

#6: Identifying the Math

Benefits: Encourages the making of mathematical connections across domains given a real world problem situation. Allows for argumentation and justification. Builds on prior knowledge.

Task: Students are asked to identify the math concepts in a given word problem by addressing the question, "What are the math concepts in the problem?"

CONCEPTUAL UNDERSTANDING

What are the math concepts in this problem?

The IKEA Mammut bed frame has a length of 66 7/8 inches and a width of 35 inches. Can this bed fit in a room that has an area of 40 square feet?

#7: Making a Mathematical Sketch

Benefits: Helps students "see" the relationships between given quantities and the context of the problem. Promotes flexible thinking, argument and justification.

Task: Create a labeled mathematical sketch to show the mathematical relationships in the problem.

REPRESENTATION

Make a mathematical sketch of the problem.

The Pizza Deal:

Angelo's Pizza has a special every Friday. You can get two large pies or three small pies for $18.00. Normally, the same orders would cost $24.00. Ashley wants to know how much more each large pie would normally cost.

Tara's Way

$24 normally

$12.00
normally

$12.00
normally

1ˢᵗ Large Pie

2ⁿᵈ Large Pie

$9.00
with special

$9.00
with special

$18 with the special

$24 normally

$8.00
normally

$8.00
normally

$8.00
normally

1ˢᵗ Small Pie

2ⁿᵈ Small Pie

3ʳᵈ Small Pie

$6.00
with special

$6.00
with special

$6.00
with special

$18 with the special

TIPs:

Label all symbols precisely according to the context.

Use lines to represent time and distance.

Use symbols like circles, squares, dots, etc. to represent objects and amounts.

Kevin's Way

Price of Pies
Friday

$18.00 L L

2 large pizza

$9.00 for each

$18.00 S S S

3 small pizzas

$6.00 for each

Price of Pies
Saturday - Thursday

$24.00 L L

2 large pizza

$12.00 for each

$24.00 S S S

3 small pizzas

$8.00 for each

TIPs:

Use a key to explain what the symbols are and only sketch the relevant mathematical information.

Organize your mathematical sketches to better "see" the relationships.

#8: Make a Math Model

Benefits: Provides structure to help students organize their mathematical thinking. Builds a students ability to depict ideas visually and mathematically at the same time. Is a bridge to connect mathematical sketches and abstract numerical expressions, equations, and calculations.

Task: Adapt mathematical sketches into math models (e.g., tables/charts, number lines, graphs, bar diagrams, area/array models, etc.).

REPRESENTATION

Mathematical Practice #4: Model with mathematics.

Compare the strategies: #7 Mathematical Sketches to these math models.

Tara's Math Model about the "Pizza Deal" problem:

Size of the Pizza	Special Deal Price	Normal Price	Difference in Prices
Small	$6.00	$8.00	$2.00
Large	$9.00	$12.00	$3.00

Kevin's Math Model about the "Pizza Deal" problem:

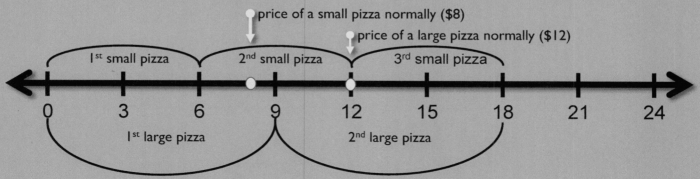

PONDER THIS!

The ability to problem solve develops slowly over a long period of time; perhaps because the numerous skills and understandings develop at different rates. A key element in the development process is multiple continuous experiences in solving problems in varying contexts and at different levels of complexity (Kantowski, 1981).

DISCUSSION OPPORTUNITY

#9: Worked Solutions

Benefits: Models different solution pathways for students and promotes flexible thinking. Deepens understanding of the problem given.

Task: Show samples that were already completed. It is best if the students have already tried to work out the problem(s) for themselves.

IMITATION

Imani and Oni want pizza. Imani has $5.00 and Oni has $2.00 less. A slice of pizza costs $1.50 or you can get two slices for $2.50. How many slices can they purchase?

Mathematical Sketch

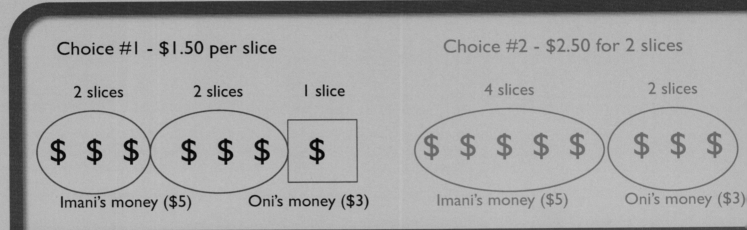

Choice #1 - $1.50 per slice

2 slices   2 slices   1 slice

$ $ $ $ $ $ $

Imani's money ($5)   Oni's money ($3)

Choice #2 - $2.50 for 2 slices

4 slices   2 slices

$ $ $ $ $ $ $ $

Imani's money ($5)   Oni's money ($3)

# of Pizza Slices	Cost at $1.50 per Slice	Cost at $2.50 for 2 Slices
1	$1.50	$1.25
2	$3.00	$2.50
4	$6.00	$5.00

Math Model

Mathematical Practice #3:
Construct viable arguments and critique the reasoning of others.

Choice #1 - $1.50 per slice

Choice #2 - $2.50 for 2 slices

$1.50 + $1.50 = $3.00 for 2 slices

$2.50 + $2.50 = $5.00 for 4 slices

(2 x $3.00) + $1.50 = $7.50 for 5 slices

$5.00 + $2.50 = $7.50 for 6 slices

Imani and Oni can get 5 slices of pizza at $1.50 per slice with $8.00, but they can get 6 slices if they take the 2 slices for $2.50 deal. With both choices they will get $0.50 in change, but with the 2 slices for $2.50 they will get more slices. Imani and Oni can each get 3 slices with the $8.00 that they have.

PONDER THIS!

A "vital" part of students' problem solving activity is **metacognition,** which includes both the awareness of their cognitive processes and the regulation of these processes (Lester, 1985).

DISCUSSION OPPORTUNITY

#10: Cloze Word Problems

Benefits: Encourages the reading and re-reading of word problems. Provides the opportunity for students to make sense of the word problem.

Task: Words are blocked out or hidden in a word problem . Students have to figure out what words are missing given the context.

COMPREHENSION

Mathematical Practice #1:
Make sense of problems and persevere in solving them.

Fill in the blanks given the context.

A _____ airplane ticket from New York City to

Atlanta, Georgia and back costs _____ $260.00.

Most airlines charge about $25.00 to check a bag. If

a family of 4 _____ to buy _____ tickets

from New York City to Atlanta, about how much would

the trip cost?

PONDER THIS!

Summarizing research efforts by the National Research Council, Resnick (1987) concluded that **reasoning and higher order thinking have these characteristics:**

1. Higher order thinking is **non-algorithmic.** That is, the path of action is not fully specified in advance.

2. Higher order thinking tends to be **complex.** The total path is not "visible" (mentally speaking) from any vantage point.

3. Higher order thinking often yields **multiple solutions,** each with costs and benefits, rather than unique solutions.

4. Higher order thinking involves **nuanced judgment** and interpretation.

5. Higher order thinking involves the **application of multiple criteria,** which sometimes conflict with one another.

DISCUSSION OPPORTUNITY

6. Higher order thinking often **involves uncertainty.** Not everything that bears on the task at hand is known.

7. Higher order thinking involves **self-regulation** of the thinking process.

8. Higher order thinking involves **imposing meaning,** finding structure in apparent disorder;

9. Higher order thinking is **effortful.** There is considerable mental work involved in the kinds of elaborations and judgments required.

Young children and lower-ability students can learn and use the same **reasoning strategies and higher-order thinking skills** that are used by high-ability students (Resnick, et al., 1991).

DISCUSSION OPPORTUNITY

#11: Numbers, Numbers, Numbers

Benefits: Enables children to read and make sense of the numbers in word problems. Guides comparison, argumentation and justification. Promotes the associating of numbers with specific units given the context.

Task: Identify and list all of the numbers in a word problem. Without solving the problem, explain what each of the numbers mean given the context.

CONTEXTUALIZING

Mathematical Practice #2:
Reason abstractly and quantitatively

List the numbers in the problems and explain what they mean in the context.

Problem A: Erin and Bonnie each collected a dozen apples when they went apple picking last Saturday. As soon as Erin got home she used 5 apples to make an apple pie. Bonnie shared half of her apples with her two siblings. How many apples does each girl have left?

Problem B: Christopher went to the gas station and bought 12 gallons of premium gas to put into his BMW. It cost $5.00 per gallon. He was very upset about the price because 2 years ago it only cost ½ as much. How much more money does Christopher have to pay now for 12 gallons of premium gas than 2 years ago?

PONDER THIS!

Student's Misguide to Problem Solving
A Joke by Lynn Nordstom

Rule 1: If at all possible, avoid reading the problem. Reading the problem only consumes time and causes confusion.

Rule 2: Extract the numbers from the problem in the order they appear. Be on the watch for numbers written in words.

Rule 3: If rule 2 yields three or more numbers, the best bet is adding them together.

Rule 4: If there are only 2 numbers which are approximately the same size, then subtraction should give the best results.

DISCUSSION OPPORTUNITY

Rule 5: If there are only two numbers and one is much smaller than the other, divide if it goes evenly, otherwise multiply.

Rule 6: If the problem seems like it calls for a formula, pick a formula that has enough letters to use all the numbers given in the problem.

Rule 7: If rules 1 - 6 don't seem to work, make one last desperate attempt. Go back to rule 2 and perform about two pages of random operations using these numbers. You should circle about five or six answers on each page just in case one of them happens to be the answer. You might get some partial credit for trying hard.

DISCUSSION OPPORTUNITY

#12: This and That, and Them

Benefits: Helps students define and clarify what pronouns are referencing in a given situation.

Task: For every pronoun (*I, we, you, he, they, them, this, that, those, its, etc.*) in the word problem, students explain what the pronoun is referring to.

MONITORING/CLARIFYING

Mathematical Practice #1:

Make sense of problems and persevere in solving them.

Highlight the pronouns and explain what they mean in the word problem context.

Shelby has 20 Pokémon cards. **This** is four times greater than the amount that **he** had last year. By how much did **his** collection increase?

Notes About Strategies

#1: Word Problem Puzzle

Implementation Suggestions:

- o   Copy each sentence on to a separate strip of paper.
- o   Use at least a size 24 font if using a word processing program.
- o   Place each puzzle set into a labeled envelope to keep organized.

Solution: Tony has 18 Skittles. Tina also has some Skittles. Tina has 6 fewer pieces of candy than Tony. How many pieces of candy does Tina have?

#2: What is the Question?

Implementation Suggestions:

- o   Multi-step problems generate more (and a wider range of) questions.
- o   Prompt students to generate "grade-level" questions about grade-level math concepts.
- o   Have students work in small-groups to answer the questions.

Solution: Answers will vary, but possible questions are:

- o   How much money did Julie spend? (5th Grade)
- o   If the sales tax was 8.25%, and Julie had $200, how much change would she get back? (7th Grade)

#3: A Line at a Time

Implementation Suggestions:

- A "line" can be a complete sentence or a part of a sentence, separated by a comma.
- Use contrasting colors to distinguish each line.
- Have students share and compare their visualizations of each line.
- Combine with strategy #5: Make a Mental Movie.

Solution: Interpretations will vary, but use the first line to establish the context. For example, you could ask the questions: What kind of park is this? Does it look like a playground? A large city park? The Grand Canyon? How do you know?

#4: State in Your Own Words

Implementation Suggestions:

- Highlighting nouns (e.g., names and places) encourages students to generalize.
- Highlighting unit amounts (e.g., 3 feet) leads students to make conversions.
- Use a highlighter to indicate words that should be paraphrased.

Solution: Paraphrasing will vary, but possible paraphrase is: Willow Smith is about **24 months** younger than her **sibling** Jaden. Her oldest brother is about six years older than Jaden. Willow's birthday is on **October 31st**. How old will **she** be when Trey turns 21?

(FYI: A) Willow Smith would be about 13 years old when her oldest brother Trey is 21 years old, because she is about 8 years younger than Trey. B) This information is true.)

#5: Make a Mental Movie

Implementation Suggestions:

- Use real-life or imaginable situations that are familiar to students.
- Use authentic materials (read: real stuff) where possible.

Solution: Visuals will vary, but students should "see" 11 students (i.e., Amir and 10 friends). Students should "see" the four items purchased (2 hamburgers, a bag of fries, and a juice) for each child, costing $4. *Some students would begin calculating by skip counting by multiples of 4 or by multiplying 11 x 4 to get $44.*

#6: Identifying the Math
Implementation Suggestions:
- o This strategy is challenging for students, because we do not often look at the math concepts, just solutions.
- o Provide students with a list of possible math concepts and have them debate which ones apply and why.

Solution: Measurement: linear measurements with Customary units (e.g., inches, feet), area, addition/subtraction, measurement conversion within a system of measure.

(FYI: A) The bed will fit. The area of the bed is about 6 ft. by 3 ft. or 18 sq. ft. B) This was an actual product sold by Ikea.)

#7: Making a Mathematical Sketch
Implementation Suggestions:
- o Mathematical sketches are specific to each situation and each student's interpretation of that situation.
- o A student looking at a mathematical sketch should be able to tell the word problem story without having to read it.
- o Have students work collaboratively to refine and revise sketches.

Solution: Sketches will vary. See pages 25 – 26, 28. Each large pie would normally cost $3.00 more.

#8: Make a Math Model
Implementation Suggestions:
- o Math Models are more generalized structures for showing/diagramming mathematical relationships for a given situation.
- o Mathematical sketches are the bridge to help students make sense of math models.

Solution: Choice of math models will vary. See page 28.

#9: Worked Solutions

Implementation Suggestions:

- o Before showing a worked solution provide students time to work through the problems independently.
- o Worked solutions problems can be ones that were previously done for homework or classwork.
- o Allow students to critique worked solutions and share how they would make the solutions better.
- o Have students work collaboratively to make a book of worked solution problems.

Solution: See pages 31 - 32.

#10: Cloze Word Problems

Implementation Suggestions:

- o Have students work in a small-group to discuss and reason through word choices.
- o A word bank could be provided as a scaffold.
- o It is not recommended to "blank out" nouns.

Solution: A round-trip airplane ticket from New York City to Atlanta, Georgia and back costs about $260.00. Most airlines charge about $25.00 to check a bag. If a family of 4 wanted to buy four tickets from New York City to Atlanta, about how much would the trip cost? *Provided each person checks one bag, then the round-trip cost would cost about $1240 for a family of four. That is: (4 x 260) + [(2 x (4 x 25)]. That means four round-trip airplane tickets at $260 per ticket, plus double four times $25, as we have to pay the cost of checking a bag bag each way.*

#11: Numbers, Numbers, Numbers

Implementation Suggestions:

- Use a problem that shows numbers both numerically and in word form.

- Longer word problems provide greater opportunities for students to really think more critically.

- Once students understand the strategy, give them a problem that has the numbers and as ask them to justify what each number means.

Solution: In the chart below the numbers appear in the order that they appear in the problems.

Problem A		Problem B	
Number	**Meaning of Number in Context**	**Number**	**Meaning of Number in Context**
dozen	*amount of apples each collected by Erin and Bonnie, so 24 apples in all*	12	*gallons of gas bought by Christopher*
5	*number of apples Erin used to make an apple pie, so she* **had 7 apples left**	5	*price per gallon in dollars, so it cost Christopher $60 for 12 gallons*
half	*amount Bonnie shared with her siblings, so she had* **6 apples left**	2	*is a reference that Christopher was making about the price of gas 2 years ago*
two	*the number of siblings that Bonnie has*	1/2	*refers to the price of gas two years ago as half as much as the current $5 price per gallon, so* **Christopher had to spend $30 more now for gas**

#12: This and That, and Them

Implementation Suggestions:

- Explicitly teach students how to recognize pronouns or when a word is referencing another word or situation.
- Use this as an opportunity to use precision in math.
- Make into a daily routine without having to solve the problem.

Solution: **This** at the beginning of the second sentence refers to the, "20 Pokémon cards" that Shelby has. **He** in the middle of the second sentence refers to Shelby. **His** in the middle of the last line refers to Shelby.

If we replaced the highlighted pronouns with what they reference, then the word problem would read as follows:

Shelby has 20 Pokémon cards. **20 Pokémon cards** is four times greater than the amount that **Shelby** had last year. By how much did **Shelby's** collection increase? *Shelby's collection increased by 15 cards or you could say his collection increased by 300%.*

of Pokémon cards of Shelby has now:

OOOOO   OOOOO   OOOOO   OOOOO

1x as much as last year   *2x as much as last year*   *3x as much as last year*   *4x as much as last year*

of Pokémon cards of Shelby had last year:

OOOOO

Shelby had 5 cards last year

FREE Online Resources

Illustrative Mathematics:

Developed by the writers of the Common Core State Standards and filled with problem solving tasks aligned to the standards. (Grades: K – 12)

www.illustrativemathematics.org

Math Playground:

A resource packed with skills-building games, virtual manipulatives and sets of worked problems. (Grades: K – 8)

www.mathplayground.com

Word Problem Error Analysis Template:

A guide to help educators identify where a student's gaps are in the problem solving process. (Grades 2 – 12)

www.ckinged.com/wpea

References

Bergenson, Terry. **Teaching and Learning Mathematics: Using Research to Shift From the "Yesterday" Mind to the "Tomorrow" Mind**. Washington, USA: Resource Center, Office of Superintendent of Public Instruction, 2000.

Web: k12.wa.us/research/pubdocs/pdf/mathbook.pdf

Hyde, Arthur A. **Comprehending Math: Adapting Reading Strategies to Teach Mathematics, K-6**. Portsmouth, NH: Heinemann, 2006.

Web: heinemann.com/shared/onlineresources/e00949/introduction.pdf

Pólya, George. **How to Solve It; a New Aspect of Mathematical Method**. Princeton, NJ: Princeton UP, 1945.

Web: notendur.hi.is/hei2/teaching/Polya_HowToSolveIt.pdf

Research-Based Strategies for Problem-Solving in Mathematics K-12. Tallahassee, Florida, Florida Department of Education, 2010.

Web: floridarti.usf.edu/resources

About the Author

Christine King is a K - 8 Math Consultant and Technology Integration Specialist with over 20 years of experience as an educator. As a Teach for America alumni, Christine adheres to the belief that all children can learn given appropriate tools and effective, research-based instruction.

Christine holds a Master's degree from Teachers College, Columbia University. She is the author of The Digits Game, N^3 No Naked Numbers, and Test-Savvy Math. Christine is an educational consultant who works with schools and districts across the country on elementary and middle school math curriculum, test-savvy strategies, technology integration for incorporating and reinforcing 21st century skills, and mathematical best practices.

In addition, Christine has provided math professional development throughout the United States working with, Math Solutions (Scholastic), The Bureau of Educational Research (BER), AUSSIE, Catapult Learning, and Newton Educational Services.

OTHER Books & Products

Contact Us

Want training on how to use these ideas in the classroom?

CKingEducation is available for
on-site workshops, classroom demonstration
lessons, and online webinars.

Call: 412-CKingEd
Web: www.ckingeducation.com
Email: christine@ckinged.com

CKingEducation
www.ckingeducation.com

Made in the USA
Middletown, DE
19 October 2017